Watering

WATERING

Catharine Savage Brosman

University of Georgia Press, Athens

For my mother, and in memory of my father

Special Acknowledgments

A number of the poems were written under a grant from the Board of Education of the Presbyterian Church, U.S., whose support I acknowledge with gratitude. To John and Judith Fischer belong special thanks for their assistance with the manuscript. I want also to express my appreciation for the affectionate encouragement of my husband, Paul W. Brosman, Jr.

Acknowledgments

The following poems originally appeared in the publications here noted: "Freshman," *AAUP Bulletin;* "Dare County" and "Payne's Prairie," *Approach;* "Peace in July," *Colorado Quarterly;* "Big Meadows in March" and "In the Restored Quarter of St. Augustine," *Critical Quarterly;* "At Crescent Beach," *Florida Quarterly;* "The Esthetic of Furniture," "Love Poem under the Sun," and "Of How the Lizards Live," *Georgia Review;* "Cardinals in Winter" and "January Oranges," *Kansas Quarterly;* "Looking for Grunions," *New Orleans Review;* "At the Snail's Eye," *Perspective;* "Carnival of Turtles," *Prairie Schooner;* "Fiddler Crabs," "From the Debris," and "The War at Crescent Beach," *Shenandoah;* "Camden House," *South Carolina Review;* "Beaching" and "A Lesson in Ourselves," *South Dakota Review;* "Frustrating Fish" and "A Question of Identity," *Southern Poetry Review;* "Cedar Key," "Consolation to a Friend for a Trip to Michigan, Not Taken," "Watering," and "Weathering at a Fire," *Southern Review;* "Last Parting," "Rowing Out," and "Tying Up," *Southwest Review;* "Still Life with Bottle," *Trace;* "15 September," *Transatlantic Review;* "Shore Life," *TransPacific* (formerly *Colorado State Review*); "After this Slack Summer," *Virginia Quarterly Review.*

Contents

Watering

1 A QUESTION OF IDENTITY

Watering

On the edge of our rise looking
outward to the ocean,
oleanders and poinsettias stand in shallow pits
threaded along the afternoon fence.

From one dirt basin to another
I pull the green ribbon of the hose,
letting a silver thread
splash the dust; then still spinning,
seek lanes and hollows,
ring the roots and rouse the dark powder;
then with a rush and a deeper gurgling
encircle high the center clump
making islands and pools, first muddied,
finally clearing enough to be blue.

Down the row the hose and I move slowly, waiting
each time for the water to rise
to the brim, while the long yellow rays
turn the brown circles behind us to opal.

When the last trench tastes
the spray on its lip and the gray stems
have grown moist up to the first leaves, I look back
to the chain of pools and droplets
where a little labor has taken root
in living things.
A gust comes up, from the sea, to whip
the diked water which quivers eagerly,
and I see how the gardener,
guessing at some dark thirst
—the wind with sea-thoughts—
writes the rings of his own desire upon the earth.

January Oranges

Graying snow stretches from the windowsill
to the hedge, the rooftops, up the hill
and to the Alleghenies' clouded line.
On the inside ledge, a potted orange tree
blossoms and bears unseasonably
its fruit—branches bangled with full
skins—and scatters through the room
heady scent. It is a dark afternoon;
an overcoated man passes, under a mud

sky, and shifts his briefcase. The shine
of the oranges bespeaks somewhere a yellow
sun, where leaves laugh in a grove
and cleaving fruits spill in the clear
light, as pickers' arms mellow.
In winter, it takes only a leaf
for knowledge, only a toy tree throwing
sharp globes of orange on the dull
surface of my thoughts; and to love

things as they are (the epiphany
when an idea comes into bloom)
only the fragility of a flower,
panes that can crack and the fear
that a branch will break, in grief
under the weight of so much growing—
or freeze one night when I forget to pull
the curtain, and let disorder devour
the delicate eyes of the buds.

Cedar Key

Salt takes us by the nose,
rising sharp from marshes
which border the last pines
and sandy palmetto scrub
of the peninsular shelf.
A blue heron soberly
edges the upland forests
with a water-mark.
Dipping along mangrove
bayous, gulls sketch
the force of the wind
as it measures how shores
lie open.

       A half-deserted
port, shaped under storm-
bent cedars, rocks its moles
loose, and its swamped hulls
scattered in the labyrinth
of keys, like old linen
put out to dry, and left.

At an abandoned factory
the outline of a giant pencil
among the unused trees
stands like the wind's steeple.
Light has bleached the docks
white as clam shells. Shacks,
with their battered palm thatch
flapping at the eaves, mark
the line of the bay.

               Places
left long stand clean,
baring their own face;
under the chipped paint lay
forgotten wood, and the smell
of cedar comes through salt.
There is a loneliness
only a hurricane leaves,
empty of all but its own
quiet and the gray features
of storm; and then comes
an age when essentials
tell, without music, their
constant endurance.

10

Noon,
at play on the water, traces
the line of the port
in brilliance. The surf
slaps these blackened pilings,
giving its green light,
and pulls our steps
over the splintered planks,
sounding. A cormorant comes
before the wind. On this
day, like all days, one
might sail out to sea—
but the endless horizons
are also here—circles of days
returning—and the port
spread naked before the sea
stays to discover itself
and hold in its weathered arc
revolving yellow suns,
all changes being a way
back to the beginning.

In the Restored Quarter of St. Augustine

Assume that these houses of coquina stone,
properly aligned in a prim sarabande,
their balconies billowing like the gowns
of iron that rib Velasquez ladies, stand

in the pale gold of a seventeenth-
century summer. Already old then, this town,
by a hundred years; the fort, newly
rebuilt, turns its five-turreted crown

to land, sea, and river, on the broad
brow that guards its Catholic chastity.
For weeks no English have come down
from the Carolina coast; the city

breathes the mild air of the Matanzas;
Spain is but a tapestry of the mind.
You drink chocolate from a copper cup,
hear mass at the mission, walk as the wind

strums the palm strings; you spend
one day each week in a vaulted room
dipping candles for endless dusks, while
the cannon watch. Hibiscus gardens bloom

long into autumn. Perhaps news will come;
a ship with French cloth; letters; wine;
officers will visit the posada, talking
of empire; and your way will intertwine

a moment with the other world; then return
to your patio, and the thoughts you spin
on the wheel of time. As it mills,
walls will alter, after you have dressed in

black, borne others to their graves,
been so laid. Yet this enduring matter
will survive the changes of its forms:
if rock crumbles, it will, in a latter

age, revive as mortar; timbers will beam
an arch that bears its sceptered ancestry
as trophies. On such homage you can dream
in the streets of the seventeenth century.

Shore Life

I
The heavens are at high
tide tonight: stars reach
to the tide's rim, stuff
all we can see of the sky,
and spill, powdery, into the surf—
splashing the beach
and turning to phosphorescent eyes
fixed on our intruding thighs.

II
By the sign "No Fishing From Bridge"
they cluster, a pole for each
and one bucket—three generations,
confident in the sheriff
and knowing that the drawbridge
slows traffic to twenty. Line
dangles onto the pavement. My morning
errands run, I return
by the same route: they have put on hats
and are squabbling
over a bleeding fish.

III

Beds of shells exude in the mud flat
as the tide falls. This evening when I crossed
the Matanzas bridge, I saw shell turds
rising from the river—scattered like ruins
of adobe, or the dung of dolphin herds
but wet, waiting to be mortar.
                                        The intent
of time is still not clear. Are they a lost
and golden age of mollusks, or the runes
from the ocean's past? perhaps we look at
the foetus of another continent
abuilding from the tidal sediment—
Atlantis of our flotsam, our frail bones
which the river's wheel turns slowly into stones.

IV

Light is collapsing at last—
a huge tent falling in slow motion,
folding at the edges
in cloudy piles. Only the marsh pines
pole up some of the day's green.
My caged fan drones with the crickets.
When the moon rises, fishermen
will drive down on the wet sand,
headlights spotting the waves
where mullet are running—

and will cast their nets,
beast to beast and trapped to trapped,
drawing in to blindness
the amber gills, the burning red eyes
which, as darkness sucks the sun,
are still pursuing their cold prey.

V

If you cannot wash the sand
from your skin, or the surf's
obscure language from your tongue,
if you cannot read the words
written on the city walls, say
that you have preferred sounds
of the ocean's bowels, to the chatter
of yard hens: that the sun, burning
above your eyelids, has left
dust from its dandelion flames
in your eyes; that, blind, you
have seen asteroids at night,
treading soundlessly across
the sandy dunes of the sky.

Tying Up

The oar arcs: cuts the surface, slices
under, slips out, to fall again
with a faint slap; and the water
freely yields to the repeated pull.

We circle in the sun, turning with
our reborn shadow as it shrinks, vanishes,
rounds once more. Within a safe pale,
coots plunge and reappear,
busying in their water-ways; and skimmers,
rootless, sketch paths for their
invisible desires. Oars dropped,
we drift with the indifferent design
of wavebeats. Behind the reeds
that hide the shore, land
and land's measured time have disappeared.

But (after noon's white sleep) the wind
wakens, moves out from the pines,
churns about under foraging clouds,
whips spray and whisks
our thoughts from the fragile husk

of the boat's hull, back
to what has been forgotten
only through the will that wrenches music
from frightening stars, and finds
a friendly eye in the black pools
of a deserted lake.

When we tie up at the dock and start
through the tangle of cabbage palms
and yucca, crowded fierce over the sand,
we leave a motionless summer dream
bobbing at the water's edge—
and shiver.

At Crescent Beach

I

This desert—where the wind shakes out its mane
and neither words nor seasons stay to tell
of time and presences, since passing wakes
have vanished like a shadow—has no name
nor memory. The tide-strewn chips of shell
remain as afterthoughts; the smooth swell breaks
but will not scar. For one to say farewell
is to forget indifference; or else
to put the changing center of his own
emotions in the huge uncentered frame
of oceans, and prefer their cruel green
to history and its possibilities.

II

When goodbyes come, they come between our eyes
and what we've looked at: I have seen the skies
fall crimson, gushing, into a dark sea
as the gulls gathered; watched the seaweed, surf-
entangled, slap the shore; shouted in the wind
which rose and trumpeted the night; and see
today this stretch of sand like a long dream,

already distant. Thus it is with love,
and with the places chosen: the wide scene
we cannot leave without leaving our mind
estranged, and curtained from itself. A stream
of whiteness blossoms from the slate-dark blue,
catching my longing in its brilliant screen,
impressing and imprisoning my view.

III

At the dunes' crest the sea oats bend to laugh
under the spilling sunshine. Whitecaps dance,
and shrimp boats perching high on the blue surf
parade like pelicans, with rigs outthrown
and nets unfurled; their ordered rise and fall
moves with the tide, and drawing in their zone
seaward desire, turns back our memory
to weathered currents. Eon-creeping, we
have left the water, chiseled wood and stone,
and laid the labyrinth of towns; but bone
recalls familiar salts, and runs away
from the expanding skies, hollows a tree,
and sails beyond the locks of circumstance.

IV

Up in the citadels of rocks and books
and proper usages, the pavement smokes
in the June sun. Slowly the crab minds move,

send predatory claws exploring, shove
aside objections, pinch and snatch at prey,
patient—planning to spend a pleasant day
in sermoning, and have a meal to boot,
and thus to save the world. A tasty way
to make philosophy their living. —Out
in the ocean porpoises make love,
and circling skimmers sing of paradise.

V

In a strange world, at the dividing line
of the opaque and massive land—sand, pine
and oak—and what moves endlessly, retreats,
returns, washing up light from Portugal,
we meet the mirror of our tidal I—
escaping in the sea, surrounding all
or orbiting like Archimedes' point
above; but bound to its own shore, beneath
the zenith. So reflection must endure
the prospect of the distance. Yet the lure
of inward images draws back our eyes
to range in time; the inner ocean beats
in echoes of the flood, and as we leave
—a double world—we breathe through the wind's breath
and read the heart's mute markings, memory.

Beaching

Beaching is a return.

At this scissored edge
where the water comes up,
we bridge a prejudice
and, sandy-toed, venture out
to stand in the shallow waves
that nip at our ankles
and to dip into a wet world—
reflection we remember.

There is more of the world in our wishing
than we know, more reaching
and running back to the swell
which pushes history windwards.
We run, without thinking why,
to the cresting breakers, throw ourselves
against their wall, drink the salt
and let the surf toss us
until we lose our balance
and tumble, rolling like a water wheel.

Whoever plays bowls
with these waves, which chase
and are chased, hides out somewhere
over the horizon. Emptied of all
but the shore and ourselves, it is not
metaphysics we find,
or the End beyond the waves'
slapping. The sun is a brassy
disc rimmed with fireworks. The sky
is blue. Skipping back to the sand,
we stretch horizontal, giving up
heights and drives:
for the end of escape
is return, and the old flat world
turns round on itself
and waits in the circle of the future.

A Question of Identity

See how the shore receded in the dark
as the tide rose: tracks of crabs
which we came to read, moon-pulled, at midnight

become cuneiform on the sea floor;
waves wash the flank of the road
and patches of grass are swallowed in the sway,

sway of water, the bubbly wreaths
visited on the drowned. Boundaries seem too
uncertain: overnight the line can change

between the loose, terrible sea
which can pull my legs out in the undertow
and the sands where I have taken hold.

My dreams of drowning revive: I can already
feel the breakers beating at my bones; old
live oaks may succumb at last to liquid.

Are all our questions still to be re-asked?
perhaps the very dryness of the land,
the wetness of the wet called into doubt?

But wait: the tide turns, and the zenith sun
sheds demarcation on the shore,
and the changing wind says   that this

is the truth of the bay:
all things must have an edge, keeping
identity, however tenuous; even space

that crashes into gaseous ruffs of stars;
oceans exhausting themselves
in shallow inlets; even a storm which is turned

back, as the trees resist. And that the ends
of things, stream, continent, or a love
splintering against a sandbar

—all peripheries—are, in their dual light,
also the center of reality—since
we know the world by differences,

the sea by the way it floods a shelf of beach,
and the wind, by its dervish shape
among antennaed dunes.

Dare County

Out of Kill Devil Hills, behind
dunes winter-ridden by the wind,
the moon treads the sound at the end of night, waiting
for the east to whiten; then
falls, rounding, into the tidewater
swamps.

       Fog gathers up its heavy
silver, and moves stealthily
over the cypress, spreading
its gray fingers. Lost
somewhere in these bogs,
ghosts begin to rattle the morning,
pulling down light among
blackened stumps, through traps
of branches. Along the single road
birds crouch shivering—silent,
in dim shapes.

So Raleigh's soul
shook here on a bare pine in the cold,
and the colony that hung their colors
beside this marsh turned slowly
stagnant, let the sand suck their feet
and their breath tangle among the ruins
of wild vines. Only whispers
from them last now, half-crazed
with all the time that has passed
and the loneliness, and the roar
of the Atlantic back there.

But what
is real—these voices out of history
or the hunter who ventures in? Truth
can be as mute as dead water,
and slugs and butterflies
have lived here happy on the decay
of trees and men. If the old fogs
of time ever lift, the swamps
will stand dazzling in the sun,
and these formless ghosts will rise
to judge all that has come after,
a long neglect of earth truths,
an ancient faith's eclipse,
and the nova years of a latter age.

Peace in July

In the long July afternoon,
the Kootenays throw their shadow against the land.
There has been planting and growing:

                                berries ripen
black, corn stands fence-high, and cherries
burst into blood against the green. Below the fir
and the grotesque running fingers of fireweed,
peaches erupt in ostentatious show, their pagan
color spreading with the sun. The earth is ripe
like a full fruit.

               In other mountains
men have carved caverns with steel doors,
and they shiver inside, in the conditioned
and antiseptic air, computing possibilities. War
spills out, like a volcano, over the planet.
This violence is old:

                    at the Hope Slide,
half a mountain fallen—rocky spittle
where earth foamed at the mouth—buries
still its dead among the ruined pines. Over
its desert, nothing. Such stillness is too sweet.
It is a question of waiting;

                              something will prick
again this obscene excretion, this belly of soil;
thunder will rupture the ridge, the granite
mountain will move, the valley will stir,
crack the hours on the sundial and frighten
the trees; and the crash

                              will lacerate this peace,
caught between the mutilations of stones
and our immemorial artillery.

Letter to Shenandoah Friends

Friends!—the word is immense,
meaning more now than it did
when I had you; learned so,
I suppose, like many things
which grow good in our minds;
so that what I had hoped to say
seems too small. Even the circles
of your apple trees
                    have left
their affection deep; and round
shadows put me in mind of those
generous fruits, and your like
nature. From this distance,
and a winter still dressed
in shirtsleeves, your valley
is a wide memory, saving for me
another winter, whose mellow
evenings still are somewhere
asleep, under the snow. What
surrounds you there

                    is soft
of contour; aromatic, as a line
of smoke moves over the ridge;
and old, a mother bear burrowing
in her fat. Without you, I
am thinned, feeling more like
a tourist tired of the sun
and taking in a movie. Forgive me
if I have drawn

                    much that you are
to my experience: it seems
that all one knows must be known
within; and that, loving each other's
lives, a moment, it is because
they have joined together. So
you remain my dream, that lasts,
where I am rich and happy,
among trees that change, properly,
at autumn, and friends in time
where they belong, lending
a sense to my long patience.

Camden House

I am standing in the kitchen,
my hair in braids around
my head. Iron and copper pots
hang above the wood range,
and a low window looks out
to the river, which I know
as if it were my blood.
He is wearing a sword
and a gray cavalry costume,
and though he does not speak
I know that the sergeant
is waiting, and that he leaves
for another war, which I
had only read about, and now
relives for me. A presentiment
of disaster must haunt

him, for he will not go;
he paces to the door, a glove
slaps, and I grow embarrassed
as the moment swells, floods,
passes.—Later, I am alone,

in the drawing room, under
yellow Italian curtains
whose huge flowers mingle
in patterns incomprehensible.
It is quiet, and I do not
breathe: then the fulfillment
comes, ever following quickly
in dreams upon fear or hope:
the shots blast. —I awoke.

So Camden—named for a lord—
got its tower blown off
by a federal gunboat
shooting blind at the head
of the South. It came around
the bend, where the Rappahannock
crooks under steep banks,
had to follow the channel
along the bluff. The gunners
could see only the corbelled
eaves of the villa; they shot,
for target practice.

She was alone in the house
then, with the servants
and slaves. She saw the cuts
where the lowest shots lodged

in the timbers of her wedding
chamber, walked among debris
in the garden. It was calm,
afterwards. No peace endures.
He had built this, across
the river from her birthplace,
to woo her over. A Baltimore
architect had come to oversee
the building; the blueprints
hung, framed, in the hall.
Three years later, he
was a colonel in a dissident
army; she was twenty-two.

Before the gunboat came,
he had bidden her goodbye.
Under the Lee and Carter
portraits, he had let her hear
not of present necessity,
but of a future, of the house
that was his love for her,
and of the long elm lanes
he would plant, where they would
pass, and their children later.
Then he walked to the boxwood
hedge, where his horse waited.

Two-minded South, two-faced:
honor and slavery, white
and black. Some still live
the wound of it. I walk along
the alleys, which a descendant
trims on his power mower. All
has once again been called
into question; I move
among the columns of Camden's
endurance, and think of what
the defeated men must have
felt, rocking on the porch
of the Richmond Old Soldiers'
Home. Something died at
Camden, but something else
was dreamt—love laying the pink
stones; we are its waking,
time's blueprints bred in bones.

Payne's Prairie

I

Flat lies this old lake, drained
—one year when the peninsula
shifted—through a sink hole
where the earth opened up.
(Younger, I would have wondered
why the core's visceral flames
did not leap out, burning
our familiar green, and us.)
Birds, nesting thick in the reeds
and spongy hollows, flush
from the ditches and rise
dark against a darkening
sky. In the summer, snakes
—strips of uncertainty in headlights—
wiggle coolly across the blacktop,
going to a different dampness
somewhere.

        The water's memory
lasts, pulling us low, lower
than pines and orange groves,
drawing us back in time

close to the sea which left
this question hanging on the land,
and all its sea marks: shells,
sand, salt springs. An old voice
calls with the brine of home.

II

In the savannah lives
an insistent form, recreating
its long, low face against
dark-wooded slopes, remembering
shore-lines and gulls who swooped
to define a surface;
ceaseless, its blood runs
—under the pronged prints
which egrets etch in the slime—
beyond longing, in its own
still, savage beating:
rising and falling, I hear it
flow through the prairie,
sung by wild irises
and the brown thrashers. Deep
around us, the prairie holds
our changes in its own,
stakes our wildness to old
waters and their unforgetting.

III

We have come here, together,
not to the remembered land
of childhood—which lies
in you like a burst seedpod,
and all its promises now
becoming form—but to the land
as it will be, after time
and these metamorphoses
of patient flooding, with signs
of all our past, and its rich
contours, and the ways
that the sand will settle now
and the rain water flow
—to the kneaded country
that has found its truth,
after the burning crust
and the sand's shifting, after
the ocean's falling, and the dark winds.

Big Meadows in March

The parapet of icicles along the drive
is melting now; beneath a murky sun
new pot holes dug by winter will be filled
with muddy slush, and the dirt road that leads
back to the campgrounds of escape must be
impassable, bogging again to sponge.

A senseless shifting of the sun has brought
the annual release; already roots
are agitating, fields are bristling with
grass in profusion waiting for the blade,
a thousand flowers showering in one night
like meteorites; in the fertility

of repetition, rivulets seep out,
sopping the trash that lingers from last year.
Some purity is lost in this decay
of ice and crystals; cracking stone turned sand,
salts into blood, the dark earth making leaves
mark the erosion of the winter's edge,

without the clear intention of a mind
that orders lines and purposes; like a bruise,
after the strain of change, the breaking up,
a marsh will spread. The human does not yield
its past so easily: our acts become
as stones, and will not die. In a few weeks

the campers will come back, pitching their tents
on the periphery, under the pines,
seeking a symbiosis with the world
less futile than the long immobile sleep
of brick facades; the same forgetfulness
that makes earth possible—old bones destroyed,

a compost pile—will lie around their feet,
while their late time, lacking a purpose for
itself, prolongs one failure to the next,
wanting economy of years and words—
a pattern in last autumn's wasted leaves—
beside the dumb abundance of the spring.

II A PLAIN TRUTH

Freshman

Daughter I never had, here as you sit,
eloquent listener, I wonder what

allows you to display upon your face
the secrets which at home you hid; what grace

can let you find in me, so much like you,
a master. Though these words you hear seem new,

what you reveal is mirror, old as love—
as all our parents, in the years when, of

a piece with you, they sat upon that row.
You are our history; in you I know

past perfect. Write the paradigm I ask:
I am listening to you, under my mask.

Still Life with Bottle

A bottle breathes blue light;
the polished eyes of copper pans are hung
questioning in a row; the onions, strung,
make a long amulet.

Across the cabinet
things idle mutely in their artifice
like poems—put in place
and carrying the stress of ritual,
but mulling over mutiny, alive
and ready to rebel; when I incline,
caught by pythonic eyes,
to contemplate again the cryptic walls,
to join my Siamese shadow on the floor
at the center of objects in repose,
I am not sure that they have exorcized
what gnaws the rib of style;

or whether, tired of being heraldry
and waiting on the side of the event
—the writing of ourselves—
they have resumed their war
as atoms in the dark. Perhaps the line
of these familiar forms will fracture, while
the images reflecting what we take
for order will dissolve
in wordless nothingness; yet she who wove
an undone tapestry
and made the bed as ballast for her love
while talking to herself could still compose
fidelity from a dumb loom, and wake
ten years with the same timeless wrinkled face
that made Ulysses smile.

The Esthetic of Furniture

Morris advised that a room contain
nothing useless, and that all function show
clearly; only, perhaps,
an Italian print as ornament,
allowing that a moral lies in the best
of design.
          The Shakers
suspended chairs and tables, lived
without any superfluity; Japanese
still eat on cushions, fold away the walls,
and, in the morning, roll
their mats.
             So what, woman,
are we doing in this flea market? Why
is that tortured vase perched
with its limp ivy on a guéridon
too small for any lunch, whose legs
get in my way? I cannot even find
my newspaper in the jumble,
and the buffet chokes with china
much too delicate, and thoroughly
out of style. Away,

                    carry it away!
let the bare floor show
and the bed be stripped
to the mattress; we will find sleep
lighter without a counterpane,
and eat to a plain truth,
Mr. Morris speaking from beyond the grave,
"He who lives simply lives in innocence."

The War at Crescent Beach

Fanned by arms of windmill aerials,
the news still comes, and hums
about, benign, with the crickets,
as its buzzing is tranquillized by

a vast light. The war is too dim
here, too remote. The dunes' thickets
tangle undisturbed in shapes set
by familiar winds, and on the sand

shore birds race the wave, dive,
return to preen. As the surf's roar
resolves all discord, I forget
exploding shells for those spread,

marking a bourn, at the tide's rim:
as if my mind were another eye
that could not stretch, sea-bound,
beyond the horizon, but like some

crab, crawled endlessly on slate walls
it cannot swim far enough to cross.
We prosper, prisoners of the shore;
and the rain, sprinkling the sound

with an artillery of useless wet,
blurs for us the faces of the war,
the shattered fields of dead
or those, shivering, still alive

who scratch with dirty hands
at the earth, among mangled limbs—
at such a distance that their loss
vanishes in the annals of the drowned.

Last Parting

Saying goodbye,
you left a cold breath blowing
in the garden, a gray
light fallen, a dull silence
in the rooms of my mind. All
that laughed yellow
one summer walked away
with you, where I cannot follow;
and now the leaves fall,
noiseless in the hollow
dusk. Tonight, I
shall keep wry company, say
wise words to the wall,
play at patience,
waiting, knowing
the winds listen, and the panes are cold.
I am old.
And that is all, all.

Consolation to a Friend for a Trip to Michigan, Not Taken

It is not exactly Frost's road:
it is not less traveled,
nor did you think that you were at
a turning point,
choosing all or nothing
with one cast of die;
and you can speculate easily enough
on the what if—
                    short, dark days;
dirty snow thumbing its nose through March;
damp treks from a borrowed apartment
to the library—
so that your curiosity is half consoled
by what you have preferred here (
magnolia leaves against a candid sky,
the redbuds popping out by Mardi Gras);

and yet there is the backside of the moon,
the lines, implicit now,
that might have come to paper on cold nights,
that unknown girl
to whom you might have had to say goodbye
one day. Even such little changes
seem immense,
                    cut into the record of
the mind. I will not regret for you,
or even make conjectures,
thinking that is yours to do—
but only say this,
that where one is, is exile, no less strange
because the reassuring sunshine rains
around the palms,
or anguish is disguised in novelty:
the adventure is essentially the same.

Michael on the Ferris Wheel

Riding on the wheel, your light
arms circling among the leaves,
you move to casual innocence,
singly complete. God's shoulder
rubs against you as you mount,

but above, the eyes of holy
fire burn, as if our celebration
must needs become the purer
flame of martyrs. What company
does our blood bear now? Since

I can no longer turn in spheres,
nor think the power your archangel
could lend you, rise; rise!
From this pained distance
that love must keep, I will wonder

at your born geometry, rounded
in a perfect likeness of spokes
and center—yet, son, should
my prayers fail, a star crash
and this ceremonial motion cease,

can you, broken, love our infirmities,
learning the hymn of practiced feet,
"We are in bodies, Lord, scattered
unto canebrakes, fallen down;
O God, gather us, separate, up."

Ancestors

Dining at Commander's Palace,
opposite Lafayette Cemetery
Number One, I face the sterile
table of the dead, spread white
behind the crumbling walls,
the stems of ornamental iron
marking the sugar mounds
of monuments, where students,
bums, tourists walk around;
have their lunch, leaning
on a rococo tomb, and taste
the wine of calm; or rest
in a sacred dusk the oaks
do not disturb. The quiet is
misleading; no one there is quite
interred, but surfaces in stone,
unreconciled with earth, apart
from all but an essential
hunger, which gapes through
the open gates. What burial
can prevail, what grass deny
such presence? Not even ritual

can contain the mystery of mind
without its lusting carnivore,
helpless in an enforced fast.
My appetite is thin, compared
to the desire of bones coveting
flesh; the ancient hurts feed,
bitter, on each other; vainly,
rivalries endure, quickened
in a common grave. However
shoring up, our dream charades
of them will not suffice, nor
that repose we prayed for:
from the marble mouths of
angels, hovering web-winged,
our sleepless fathers,
sucking at our memory but
sinking in the spongy soil,
cry out to us: Eat, eat!

III A BESTIARY

Carnival of Turtles

See the balloons blowing out to sea!
The great turtles have crawled
onto the beach, laid their eggs under a full

moon, and sprawled
inert from exhaustion; across the dunes
come the turtle men from the University,

mark a dozen shells and attach balloons
which rise like montgolfiers.
Now, swimming with the tide,

the turtles must ride
the surface, and for miles
they will be seen,

set against the gray,
by impartial eyes
mapping the currents' pull

and their mysterious routes. But to follow
them farther, after science is satisfied,
would be truly to do turtles praise:

then, guillemots and albatross
will spy globes off the isles,
red, blue, canary yellow;

fishes will rise
from the waves; dolphins will jump alongside
in a merry-go-round of green

to celebrate the carnival at sea. Weary moths,
blown out too far, can pause,
their wings quivering from surprise,

on the smooth crest of the balloons
which send their signals by cross
winds and bob free,

blooming on the waves for all eternity
and tracing their ways
for the Great Lover of Turtles.

Of How the Lizards Live

Of how the lizards live
in the mimosa, which droops
over the terrace in heavy
solstice sun, I do not yet
know enough.
                    Since spring
I have watched them run,
pause with puffed throat
on a branch; head turned,
search with protruding eyes
that stop—or do they?—
on me; then scurry along,
light striping them
under the leaves.
                    One
drops to the banister,
weaves crazily among
fallen brown blossoms
in the gutter, skirts my
chair legs; then is gone

in a green wiggle, before
I can ask what bugs
he especially relishes
(but later, I will know!)
or tell him
          why always
—being ignorant of great
causes—I have preferred
the smallest things,
finding a sweeter pathos
than in any Götterdämmerung
among the bluets hidden
in the grass, vulnerable
pine seedlings, or a coquina
shell drained by an oyster
driller—the sun did not
blink—and cast aside
to dry in its loneliness.

At the Snail's Eye

After the morning tide
has carried in the snail,
rocked in his hard house,
and stranded him half-buried,
he nudges against the sticky
grains, and noses out
timidly toward the dense
world. Its cruel brightness
dazzles; he had known green
in the shadowy water,
but not these piercing dune
grasses, sharpened on the sun;
nor, water-locked, seen
how bare yellow sands lie
brilliant—a junk heap of stars—
stretched to noon's edge.
Alone. Only chipped clam
shells parched by the summer
recall the grief of the lost,
of the single, of those
intended for a comfort
that is gone.

The hours
and the sun are still. He
has nearly forgotten the fish
that swam by, trailing
color, the tall dancing weeds,
and the feel of the salt
flowing in him; this land
seems harsh, and the inverted
emptiness is a fierce
question, where skimmer
gulls swoop over the dunes
with a menace, crying
"Who? Who?" as if ripped
from the rushes. —So small
to confront the wide day,
so separate, left at time's
core, the snail waits
through hot hours, in drying
sand.

Quietly, fresh winds,
quickening since the tide
turned, blow the sand in fine
ridges; a shadow lengthens.
The snail emerges, head
spiraling free, and finds
the tiny water-marks
time printed on his shell
repeated everywhere; even
a salt flat ripples with
familiar arcs. Until
the evening's waves come in
to rescue him, he turns
his jewel eyes, and meets
his image in the universe.

Looking for Grunions

Poles, washtubs, nets, seines, gunny sacks
and a flashlight—as though we were afoot
to catch every creature in the ocean—
we troop down, banging and chattering,
over the shell road, the dunes, to the beach
where the tide is touching its peak.
Someone steps on a broken shell, squeals,
and we dash into the water, weapons ready.

Soon I have tangled a seine around my own
feet. The full moon has eluded us in clouds;
the waves are empty, the tide recedes.
We, not the grunions, have been fooled;
they are not swarming on the beach, mating
with drunken disregard, as the almanacs
predicted; they are not even hiding

in the phosphorescent tongues that touch
our thighs; toes are insufficient bait.
Somewhere, the grunions hesitate, in dark
hollows beyond our nets, outwitting five
adults, four children, and the impelling
calendar. That they will not appear tomorrow
fried, on our cocktail table, with a mayonnaise

I can only applaud, grunions being most
excellent in their own element, adapted
to swift motion in the surf; but what
of their moon-pulled mating cycle, the sand
that is waiting for their summer eggs,
that impulse to come in, spawn, perhaps die?
Of love or of survival, I cannot say
whether they have chosen the better part.

Encounter with a Common Bird

That old air-conditioner is a droner;
but, silenced for a cleaning and repair,
it chirped when we pulled back the case,
and something rustled at the window frame.

Again, a chirp. Hands reaching carefully
around managed to feel the movement,
then the form, of a nestling without nest,
and—bones unbroken—draw it through

like a prize. Its body, featherless
and drab, humped in my palm; since
it was too young to fit the pictures
in a field guide, we just called it

"Bird," *Shiver on Summer Mud.* Boxed,
and carried quickly to the college lab,
it took up residence among jars, diagrams,
and the skeletons of kindred species,

and was fed—quite properly, to judge
by results—at the hands of a sophomore.
We stopped by to see it later; half-
grown, it traveled on her shoulder,

fluttered to and from its box, to show off
wings readying for the cats. Still plain
as dust, at least it met the standards
for a sparrow. By now, it has been freed,

and flies somewhere through city trees,
meeting other sparrows, and making do;
a mother bird, brooding in our oak, might
be grateful, as I am, for broken machines.

Frustrating Fish

Construct a cement aquarium,
large corneal peepholes where the liquid looks
of goldfish, dissolving in the green element,
meet your eyes through glass;

pipes, dials, tubes, and graphs
aligned on the outside walls; a needle
tracing for voyeurs the wavy repercussions of
a backbone's flip, a gill's

throbbing against a magnet; neither
sand, nor grass wiggling from white-pebbled
bottoms, but concrete and metal bounding the world
for a score of fish. Its axis,

the bar of a jungle jim
with electric nodes. The fishes' neat-nosed
curiosity, their nudgings, sharp impatience,
their silent hanging in

the water, all are watched.
Slowly, they are being starved for a conclusion;
teased to recoil, fatigued, then drawn
one by one into a maze

at eye level. Trapped
as the gates fall shut behind them, hungry
but more enraged, they follow an elusive bait
into one blind slot,

then another, turning
in tight ellipses, in maddening s's. Under
the charges they cringe, sweat cold fish sweat,
as the labyrinthine choices

suck them in; while eyes
outside watch, goading the delicate skins,
the spotted undersides, closing sluices on the free
passage of tails and fins.

Cardinals in Winter

Riding the wind on a bare mimosa branch,
or among the dun of oak leaves and dead grass,
they are the last fruit of the disappearing year,
sheltering southward its bloody remnants.

They peck briskly at the pyracantha berries,
ruffle the spider's work, find shriveling
acorns, and startle white insects that stay leaf-
hidden from cold rain. The sky has the same

pallor, as though there had come no advent
light, but only the crimson of poinsettias
and birds, reddening men's indifferent
sleep, as a child's blood stains the road

where war passes. Calling persistently,
the cardinals herald the green irony of spring,
when, happy, they will shake their winter habits,
mate several times by the second equinox, keeping

us in feathers and in song for another year
on this sweet sponge-earth; where perhaps our love
for them can intend some small appreciation,
a simple salute of one species to another.

Woodchucks

Six birches stand by the road
yonder, holding a thin line
against the pressing town.
Most of the birds moved on
when the last poplars fell,
run through by the buzz-saw,
and the woodchucks became history.
I remember one, that scampered
too late from his sunbath
on the road; though time passes,
some things stick in your mind.

Fiddler Crabs

For Ed and Betty

They creep out onto the strand again,
now that the rising tide is lapping
at their burrows near the jetty;
striking their fellows, they swarm
obscenely over the taut, wet sand,
sidestepping their way below
the concrete berm, which the inlet

will lick within the hour. If
this crawling sense were music,
I would laugh; since it is fright,
indecision hurts, as this way, that,
they do the dance of hesitation,
patternless motion at the threat
of each new wave. Such animal

desperation goes beyond history.
Dizzied by their scurrying, my mind
seeks a retreat, and follows those
who finally find caves of cracked
cement, take lodgings between rocks;
who dive blind under the broken
ledge, to wait there a tide-year

until the cataclysm ends. My bones
make a shelter in their darkness.
Survive, survive. One might outlast
even one's enemies. But private
compulsion only preserves us for
an immemorial use, among multitudes
prospering mindlessly. When the tide

falls, the sequel to retrenchment
is debacle; the fiddlers pile out
as if half-crazed, male-claw
pinching wildly, testing the sand
down toward the bubbly edge,
where scavenger blue crabs feed,
fattening on an army's remnants.

IV A LESSON IN OURSELVES

Love Poem under the Sun

You are, are, are, are, *are*, love!
I cannot get over it. The bright sun
which, granted, takes longer strides
than you, is such a familiar friend,
wheeling through most of my days
that, though he calls considerable
attention to himself (outdoing it,
sometimes, with his scarlet goodbyes)
scarcely do I accord him more
than the usual wonder
                     —but you!
daily, you make an apparition,
as if you had disappeared,
not for a night, but for years,
and then came, prince from the woods,
shedding your disguise of leaves
and sleep, and announcing, "Love me,
Princess; I will light up your eyes
like the noon sky; you will circle
all around me, and yet *I* will rise
and set for you; and no Copernicus
ever will discover which one
of us is center to the other."

Watching You Sleep

What landscape, Love, are you exploring where
I cannot follow? You have disappeared,
leaving your form; perhaps, with other feet,
treading the under surface of the world,
moving through woods that I will never know.
You leave me what is mute: bed, ceiling, lamp;
our recent words are mingled with dust motes
each time your body shifts. Who are you, absent?
Hero again, you may be riding far,
deep into history, mooring at shores
of memory, naming the nascent things;
and more yourself than when you were with me.
I wait. No matter; love will waken soon
enough. Do not conceal your secret then,
and I will kiss the god, the conqueror,
who winnows language from the stuff of dreams.

A Lesson in Ourselves

After the storm you took me by the hand
and led me to the shore. We watched the waves
—still broken—chopping at the docks, while clouds
pushed northward with the wind, and a thin light

spread low like a pale banner through the sky
which rain had rinsed. We walked along the beach
where it grows narrow, climbed up where the dunes
are battered by the hurricanes each fall

and stand half-crumbled, building with the tides
but soon eroded and losing again
their vines and grasses. Jellyfish lay dead
in purple stains, and shells I touched, still damp,

made streaks of mud and seaweed on my hands.
You showed me how the water left its mark
on all: wet patterns in the sand, the crabs
that lay abandoned near the dunes, the sea

locked back in a low place. Why do we go,
we who love one another well, to see
the passions of ungentle weather: sky
still heavy, creatures torn out of their home,

and, not far from our doorway, land ripped up
by the familiar waves? It is a play
on themes of our own love—our coming here
after another storm, the patterned world

emerging from two minds, the signs which we
would leave. It is a lesson in ourselves,
for even as we hold this happiness
in the fresh light, we feel the wind of change

within, which, noiseless, moves as oceans move
and draws me through a slow-eroding time
where all my love cannot hold you apart
from darkness gathering over the sea.

Rowing Out

When you stepped back,
I could not hold the light
fading from your eyes.
The knot undone, your oars
quick, you retreated without sound,
and as the backwash slid around
the pilings,
the outline of your face
blurred against the water.
I could not keep
even the feel of your hand,
even the smart of the rope
loosened again. The slack
of all goings frees the leaver,
letting love dissolve
and releasing half-held ties
that dangle on the sand.

After this Slack Summer

Captive along sands
where only ripples remain
—becoming dimmer—
from the keel
which ploughed when spring
and winds were rising (four hands
tight together on the wheel)

how will we sail again,
how will we find our south?
Words have turned wary
in my mouth,
and the useless spars
list. I have thrown away
my ropes, forgot the stars.

Now, the arc of days
decreases; we swing
ignorant toward the storms.
Autumn will be chary
of her sun, and will bring
bitter rain. Today,
today I have empty arms.

84

15 September

It is not right, this
separation, no one
will make me think it
—only
we must divide
somehow,
letting the rain fall
over the rocks between us,
admitting
that hours have had
the better of us,
though they hung limp
last summer;
and we must meet
distance
with a steel eye,
knowing that distance is
born in us—

but I do not like
the tireless sound
of the rain.

From the Debris

I finally wrote to him:

"Wet pine hangs in the night
when August stops still
and the lake pants hot
in its mooring. The summer
flowers are mostly gone,
and we planted nothing for
the autumn. Since you left,
I have not played my guitar

once, nor drunk gin under
the mimosa. Perhaps you have
forgotten how the lights
on a humid evening here glow
with our past clinging, sticky,
to them, and how you left words
everywhere, worn into the very
walls; sometimes they brush

me, as I pass, and the moist
breath startles me, as if your
promises had stayed to keep
me company, and I did not
have the season to wait out
alone. Often I wonder what
to do with all your fine looks
lying around." No breeze

came up for days, and I
could not expect an answer.

Weathering at a Fire

Throwing what we would forget
into the scuttle, and lying
on cushions, we watch a fire
catch and ripen.

        In a recess
where the logs sing to themselves
with a slow sizzle, ember eyes
look out at us, with the wet
cedar popping and oozing an
oily odor.

        Somewhere there, in
the cave of coals, our desire
lurks—back in the animal land
when the lion purrs at the lioness,
sick with love, and provisional
couples hunched around a fire,
growing hungry for food and love,
draw closer.

        Is it this memory
aroused, shearing me of
the necessity for words and forms
and the costumes that disguise
us, of even the awful foresight

of tomorrow? I recognize the other
man and woman we might be,
listening to the crack of wood
on the near side of warmth
and possibility.
        Somehow
("Woman," you say to me, "lovers
can ride up those flames
and wheel in each other's arms
through smoke this very night")
somehow the common lot—whether
it is this fire, or another—
seems more than adequate—

                         a grace
ample enough to reconcile
ourselves and all that cannot be—
and the weathering of time is good
when we can be nameless
as the sunken stars—while
the simple wind whines at the wall;
stripped of our masks, we face
even the loss of last year's love,
even the pride, the dying.